For more
AF.FORD BOOKS
releases, scan here.

For information:
AF.FORD MEDIA, LLC
15826 S LaGrange Road, Ste. 265
Orland Park, IL 60462

BOOKS
An Imprint Division of AF.FORD MEDIA, LLC

Printed in the United States of America

979-8-9880203-4-9 (print) 979-8-9880203-5-6 (ebook)

Cover design, illustrations, and interior design by
AF.FORD MEDIA, LLC

how to be
lowKEE

& still
write
things
when
you're
a
leftie

Hakeela Buford

 **BOOKS**

Preface 1 – Body (At a Place, Any Place):
Here we go.

...

Preface 2 – Mind (*Still* Outside):
Can I go home?

And also never commit to this again?

Preface 3 – Heart (Back at Home):
I can't believe I'm actually going through with this,

But

Here's to all of you
who helped me
because you knew I needed it,
who helped me
even when you didn't know it
(and tried to do the opposite).

And here's to hoping that
due to all of that
this helps you,
too

To
finally mute that voice that has been telling you not to
and finally do the opposite

because you need to.

But

This isn't a memoir.

But

it is.

locations to be lowKEE:

(Now, The Real) Preface

My childhood consisted of middle fingers to musty teachers, lunch fight suspensions, and butt whippings on a pretty consistent 'every two to three months' basis for said middle fingers and lunch fights up until I was about eleven.

But, no, don't worry. It's not as bad as it sounds. There were lots of hugs and powdered donuts.

And most importantly, along the way, I grabbed some nicknames. Boo, Keela Girl, Quita Boo, KB, Tequila, Keela Chila (I'm actually stuck on who called me this...), KeeKee (self-penned back in the Lil' rapper craze from my early 2000s childhood), Keela (the widely known one), and Kee.

Then, at some point during that time, I learned how to be lowKee.

Which now has me in the present: Starting to figure out how to unlearn a bit of that...

Introduction

As you can tell by this book's title, I like to play with words. It was something of a natural desire that I *had* to do as a kid with a thousand ideas. Then, it soon became something I had to do (because I *had* to).

From finally moving away from Barney stuffed animals at the age of five to... "Five times whatever" times tables while counting how many times I ducked under my third-grade classroom tables one day to avoid a slew of rulers and erasers (I guess my classmates just wanted to practice their counting, too.). To landing at the foot of various schools thereafter. I quickly learned that knowing how to word things would be my way to keep going. And knowing how to move.

Writing clever on paper and speaking clever on tongue (by wisely not sharing...and only sharing in a crafty way when I would) became my two unassuming weapons to slash away any new potential threats. To allow me to slickly infiltrate...but still, keep a bit of evasiveness.

And it worked.
I transformed from the different girl to the different but funny girl...while still kinda just doing my own thing.

And that's probably why, even still, my words couldn't lead me. Couldn't take care of it all for me every single time.

And they still can't now.

And I'm learning to navigate that better. Now, as I begin that journey, I'm doing something I've never done before.

That is, I welcome you to join me.
As I try to move from one place

on the outside

to a new place...

The Places Where

We Land Soft

...Hopefully
& Other Intimate Spaces

Ring Cam Shows Me There's a Child Outside Alone Coming Down My Street

2024

What do we do with
The Child who's without a
Child

Hood?

The Child without
A Child
's
Joy,

The Child without
A child
's
Innocence,

Moved away with
The child
's
Hood.

What do we do with
The Child
As the child
Wanders and
Wonders,
Who will let that child in?

Will it be you?
Even though that's
Definitely *not*
Your child,
You don't have one,

3

how to be lowKEE

You have one
But currently away,
Or long while lost one
To time or age.

But even still,
Will
It finally
Be
You?
Peeking out there
In your carefully decorated home,

If so,
What will you do
When that child roams,

Opens that closed closet
And sees the real mess
You've now moved them
In?

Put the child
Back out there,
To go without

Again?

Love Notes

2024

In various places,
At some point in time,
We've all had at least one
In our possession,

Even when they're not on paper.

Just means we might have to look for them a bit deeper,
And we'll find they've been
There in someone's speech,
Faces,
Hands.

Here are mine:
One I wrote
On paper, a wide-ruled lined version,
My Juliet version,
Just without a Romeo.

But my first-grade teacher didn't like that type of English,

And neither did the one
Who received
The love note.

Saw it all on her face,
Didn't need the words,
And definitely not any hands,
To get her point across.
Saw it all in her face
On that long walk of shame
Down the school corridor

how to be lowKEE

For home
That
That day I knew wouldn't feel like it
For the first time in my life
(With many more times to follow).

And I also knew
That was the last time,
Of my first time,
That I'd ever write
Another love note.

But the kids in my class had a good laugh,
The punchline ending with a punch to the gut:
Landing that night in the hands, or in this case,
Into the ears of my mom.
When she first answered the phone,
She couldn't understand.
Then when she asked me about it,
She really couldn't.
A call about

The love note.

It's *always* love notes.

Sometimes, a mutual exchange
And other times,
Landing in that harsh Land of Forbidden Fruit.
Or another time...

My sister slid a few
To me.
Right around the time
I started slipping moss of the sea and pea protein
Into my groceries.

That night,
While getting my pillow fluffed just right
I felt something underneath it.
Felt like skin, chicken,
Looked and it was a wing.
I hadn't forgotten what it looked like, smelled like
Too soon.
Of course, I didn't when I've always similarly had skin
And always wished
For wings
Of my own.
Looking back on it,
It was all probably just love.

Looking back on it,
She probably thought she was just helping me,
A little wing
To my old and newfound aims at fulfilling dreams.
Guess, with her always being the type to look for deals,
She figured it was something like
A buy one (for yourself),
Get one (from someone else who doesn't quite understand):

Love.

My mother slides a bit
Of it
My way, too:
A praise and worship service link in my email every other Sunday,
"Just to see your uncle's face up there like you're in the pew."

With the occasional footnote
If I look closely:
"But do *you* pray for you?"

To which I say,
I used to.

how to be lowKEE

To which I say,
I usually do—

But most days,
Most times
For my mom,
My sister,
My brother,
My nieces,
My nephew,

And the rest
Is self-

Explanatory.

It's not about self,

Never been.
Always been

About love.

And right before she left,
My Granny rubbed some for me
On her belly.
The words
I was already starting to not make out,
The face
Soon to be washed out
By a last breath about to land,

But the hands
Told me all:
It was love

In the chuckles
At my latest child antics that didn't impress a woman
Who'd raised eight,
It was love
In the brushes of my baby hairs,
It was love
In the claps and patience
As she'd listen to any new 'song' note I wrote,
It was love
Even when she'd no longer be around
To brush
Or to clap.

The only person in the world
To have never needed to show me with those hands,
No more than a brush
Or a clap,
Never a hit.

Because what was understood,
Didn't need to be explained any other way—
Our love lang
Uage.

So the last act
Was a touch on her belly
For me—
Even though, she'd have to leave me early—
To always
Remember that it was always

Love.

Always was,
Always has been,
Always will be,

To infinity.

More infinite than

Heartbreak.

But sometimes,
I can't help but wonder
If she were still here,
If she'd still
Understand.

Or if

I'd have to write some more,
After saying I never would
Ever again.

Woman (No Cry)
2024

No,

None of us signed up for this.

No,
...Maybe

Some of us actually did.

But
Either way,
The (biological) fact remains:
Someone's gotta do it.
And for that,
Each of us,
Whether it was voluntary or
Just an act of facing it,
Are brave as hell.

It's like enlisting in the army,
A constant war
That's been there from the start,
It seems.
If it's not the war your own body puts you through,
It's the war someone from the outside places on you,

On your body.

And somehow, still expected
For it
To be soft.

how to be lowKEE

But it no longer is,
And but,

It is.

A constant war,
Being told to

Be
Soft
When you don't want to be,

And then,

Not
To be
Soft

When you don't want to be.

And if you talk
Bad
About it,
About putting
Your body on the line,

You have to be reminded
Of your service.

Sometimes,
Soft.

But

...No.

This Trip in the Land of Forbidden Fruit is No Longer Fun.

(A.K.A. Witness How I Clearly Hadn't Gotten Over Some Heartbreak/Emotional Bullshit Yet at the Time That I Wrote This, But I Am Learning to Because I Realize That Every Experience in Life is a Spiritual Lesson and Journey Even If It's a Hurtful and Painful One and You Just Want to Whoop Someone's A__. But Hey, You Were Only In Your Twenties, So It Was To Be Expected and You Live and You Learn.)
2020

Working at this one logistics spot, I went to Thailand around this time.

Heart on the gear. Check.
No seatbelt. (Because eff it, I'm about to crash anyway.) Check.
No deeper thought
(Or self-respect or greater wisdom that starts around 27/28),
Just ready at the green light. Check.
Check

The rear views:
All kinds of forewarnings I passed by. "I told you so."
All kinds of intuition. *I told me so.*
But I still go, so

Check.
Start the engine.

The destination is Thailand.
Where mangoes, 7-Elevens, and lady suits are everywhere,
But there are no durians (because they're against the law).
And there are no truths (because it's against your the law).

Never any truths.
No...

This isn't Thailand.

Honk-honk!
Welp, gotta continue. This road stops for no one.

Cars keep going. Cars driven by bodies keep going.
Bodies keep going. Lives
Keep going past

7-Eleven number 1...

I thought I saw someone who looked like you.
But it was just an illusion, too quick of a glance,
And just as quick of a disappearance,
To really know if it was even really real.
Just like you.
I might would have said, "Let's hang."

Whoops. I did.
But I'm just an 'office friend,' right?

So why am I even on this trip?

I should've never signed on to this.
But it's too late because now I'm far too intrigued, too deep
In.

Who ever knew a smile turned into two from the corner of one's eye
Could be a passport
Into one's most intimate land?
More remote and murky and undiscovered than the land of the Sentinelese?
And much more dangerous I've come to find.

Damn.

7-Eleven number 2...

I thought being an island full of forbidden durian,
Of dragonfruit, and of passionfruit
Would be enough passion,
Would be enough to make you want me to stay.
But I'm too small, I'm too sunny, I'm too sweet.

What more did you expect from an island?

What more did you expect from someone fruity?
That's all I can bear.

Nah. You need a bad boy (That's where your 'friend' steps in.),
Not a bad boi.
And most definitely *not* a *good* boi.

When will
I see?
The ride will still take a bit longer...

Start the engine again.

The destination is
A street
That looks mad familiar.

7-Eleven number 3...

Remember I said we weren't in Thailand.
So why am I still seeing so many damn 7-Elevens?

Maybe we never went anywhere,
All confusion and cloudy thought from things
Like your BS.
Or glycemic mango smoothies.
(Damn you, Thailand.)
I don't know where I am on this trip
Or who I'm even with on this trip.

7-Eleven number fou—

Wait.

This is fucking
America.

This street looks like one I've driven before
Because

It
Fucking
Is.

It's the road I travel every morning.

Shit.

I'm going to work.

Nah. *No* good morning.
Let me clock in first.
Okay, now here.
Take this crappy, illegal, fraudulent passport
With the smile you got me to pose in like they do
Vulnerable babies in their first photo shoots
In this backwards world by smiling and silly faces on your end.

All of this was a pose:
The fake journeys promising me a good time with you,
Like concerts to hear the one voice we both liked, and
Unspoken statements within lingering eyes after hellos,
And humdrum goodbyes after walking out for the day,
All of it saying that you wanted me to be there with you to stay
Until 5
Because you got off at 5.

On your fake journeys.

You only really venture out for food, booze, and attention.
You're like a drunken tourist who gives everyone else (morning after)
Headaches by messing up their orderly mental domains,
Except sadly, you're the tourist in your own land.

But before I wisely realized that,
I jumped right into the first adventure in your land
and said, "Hello, hola yo habla Español. And see,
I can also speak
Tai-Kadai. Yup, all 74 of them."
Then you said, 'Cute, but it's guacamole, not guac. And I
Actually only speak superficiality not Thai.
And all I want to see are the fun times you can give me
While you're here.'

Damn.
All the quick crash lessons, body language 101
Were a bust.
Don't you know how damn hard this was
For me when I can't even roll my Rs?
When I can't even bear most times to communicate
How I feel about anything, let alone about anyone?

You know what? Where's your other friend?
An office friend can't go anywhere with you beyond the office anyway.
Why was I dumb?
I was so dumb.
I've never done anything like this before.
I never did any of this before.
This was the first moment of intuition that I ignored.

Something about Black Moon Liliths (you, the master) and Priapus
(Me, the slave to your allure that I had to visit) conjunct
Over palm tree-laced sunsets, IBCs and tote wrenches, and small talk.

Shame on our stellar astrology.
(Stellar karmic, *not* stellar harmony.
There is a difference; not all chemistry is good.)
That was the main attraction of this whole trip
Turned power trip.
But even more,

Shame on me.

But you won't fool me twice.

7-Eleven number 5...
No.

Make that Culver's.
I always mistake frozen ice for Slurpees.

They're basically one in the same.

Just like I mistook your attention-seeking for connection.
Now I see that they're basically one in the same.

So, back to Culver's
And then, back to the office.

Italian ice in my hands from yours
With a smile, not a cherry, on top.
Because there's no ice cream
For this vegan right here.

There's no authenticity given
For this naïve vegan right here.

Why'd you have to smile?
Why'd you have to be so damn persistent
And so damn attractive
To one who was so damn aloof
And so damn loving it
When you were so
Damn taken?
You were
So
Damn
Trifling.
And a scam.

And you still are.

7-Eleven number 6...

Is this an immigration test?
Trying to feel me out since I just stepped in
My new desk residence just a door down from you?
Saying my handwriting's not good enough.

Sorry, are you customs?
Saying my pistachios you're not adopting into your culture's diet.
So, that's why you called me into your office for the rest of yours?

And ending it all with saying, 'You dropped this.'
My heart
That you charmed
Out of its wits,
Which is more harmful than out of clothes.

Because more than baring your body,
It gets you showing your soul.

Then you strip searched it,
Made completely naked
With your baton
Opening up old wounds of past distrust
That I was finally beginning to turn back into trust,

And opening up new wounds just
For the hell of it.

Just
To see
If we all really do bleed
The same color red—even strangers.

No, correction—
You did it all in the name of 'protecting your land'

That I discovered
Was littered
In all of your own unhealed old wounds.
Just a dirty place really

Behind all of those travel brochures
Known as photo filters and your lure.

And then after you had enough of my heart's visit,
You petted it,
Only to bring it back in its now half-torn clothes.

Not even a single Band-Aid or, shit, at least some peroxide.
So that it all could bubble out
Just like this heat between us that bubbled over
Then killed the fire.
Leaving the reality: Just smoke
And mirrors.

But regardless, you came presenting this war-battered heart
Like you were the hero and not the assassin
And said, 'Here, you dropped this.'

All once again with that smile
After having me go naked.
And the crappiest part of all of this is
That moment wasn't even literal sex.

Never even went past first base.
Never even went past this office.
Damn, I was so dumb.

The next destination is...
I don't know

Where you want to go.
Don't think you even know
Where you want to go.

This isn't what I thought it was.
I was so bamboozled, never thought this would happen to me.
I'm usually good at dodging these things.
None of these places,
None of these faces
Are what I thought they were.
And now I see,

I'm not what I thought I was.

I was never a blocked, independent, lone wolf roaming on earth.
I was just a tourist in your land, in your car,
That old, rusted car.
A detoured passenger you picked up because you saw that
I wasn't really sure where I was going.
Just like you.

But the difference was that you had the car
That after all those years of use,
You'd learned how to maneuver
Even when it was barely running
On power,
On truth.

But deceiving is not my style,
And now I *do* know where I'm going.

I'm going home

That passes by 7-Eleven number 7...

And no, I'm not following you anymore.
Because you have that car of yours to drive,
You have your own family to go to,

And we don't speak the same language.

If you hear these 2 words, Run DMC (Trust me.)

2023

I'm not 'secretive'
Because I want to be 'mysterious' or 'hard to read.'
I'm 'secretive'
Because "I don't trust y'all fools."

With anything.

If someone hits you with a 'Trust me,'

Hit them with a "Trust *me*.
I don't."
Because next, you'll be hit with a
Slap in the face,
Stab in the back,
Cold ass pillow on the other side of the bed, or
A wire transfer of $5,700 that you'll never be able to
Explain to feds who show up on your front door.

Not talking from experience on the last one
(Because I dodged that 'job' instantly), and hopefully,
I never have to.
But other 'lesser' experiences didn't have any less of an impact
And a lesson
That taught me one thing:
Trust, ya gotta earn it.

Not with words
But with steady, solid (sketch-free) actions.
Otherwise, you just have a mouthpiece in your circle,
And that right there is just annoying.

Because nothing's worse than a talkative lie on two legs.
And if you don't believe me, just ask the politicians. Just ask your ex.
Or better yet,
Just ask *that* one who told you,

how to be lowKEE

"Trust me."

Shouts Out to the Ones with the Dashing Smiles Who Capture the Ones with the Growing Wings

2020 (updated in 2024)

First of all,
Thank you.

Thank you for your charm that turned out to be webs
To catch unassuming bugs,
Those you like droning around you
In unabandoned, increasingly dizzy states.

Thank you for taking us on a journey we just *knew*
We'd never be on like those other ones
Down there,
Until we suddenly found ourselves
Down there.
A journey to hell and back

That we never knew we wanted

But our souls did.

It hurt like shit.
Damn, we even have to maturely admit,
We might've shed a bit.

But we picked ourselves up,
Because who else would?
Who else can
When we're morphing
From one skin into a python?

And at the end of our long journey,
We say thank you
As we look back at our even longer, curved,
Winding, potholed roads

how to be lowKEE

We've now traveled,
That we had to travel
In some hard-hitting ways.
In ways that we needed

And probably never would have
If we'd never fallen from being butterflies
And still found enough beauty in ourselves
To slither back up.

And probably never would have
If we'd never fallen for
That smile.

IKYFL (IYKYK)

2024

I know you think this message is about to be something else

Because

I know you,

For real.

I know you for light

I know you for luck

I know you for life

I know you

For love

I know you thought this message

Was about to be something *else*

Because

I know you

Word of Advice on Heartbreak

2023

As I came across a post online by a 20-something-year-old the other day

Crying about this being her first heartbreak:

Just put some ice on it;

It'll be aight.

But

When you're finally ready.

Don't forget

To give it once again

A little heat,

Or it will become too stiff.

Because often we forget,

Our heart is a muscle.

And if you don't use it,

You lose it.

Gym

Hard Work

I know I'm not the only one...

2023

Sometimes, I just keep my earbuds in
While still having three more sets left
Even though I have no more battery left (in both respects).

With the hopes of not having to make conversation,
The earbuds' power magically resurrecting to drown out this gym music,
Or having the voices of God, Buddha, and Gandhi divinely intervene through my Bluetooth,

So that I can miraculously live through

These last three damn sets.

And possibly everything else
That will come after.

Kettlebells
2024

Sometimes, I *have* to feel the burn,
Not just in my heart, but in my arms, chest, legs.

Sometimes,
I swear it's fire.

A transformation
In the makin,

Which is why I love kettlebells.

And why I hate kettlebells.

I like to work against myself, I guess.
I like to work myself, I guess.

Work this mess
Into
Definition,
A mess
Turned into

A masterpiece:
A thicker skin
After a good bruise
Life has slapped on my wrists,
And that I think
I might've become accustomed to.

It's probably a bit morbid,
A bit tough,
But that's what good work

Outs feel like most days,
Especially with life.

Especially with all of its kettlebells.

Because once the skin finally toughens,
And the chest, arms, legs follow suit,
And you're on fire,

Man.

Once the skin finally toughens,
And the chest, arms, legs follow suit,
And

you're

still

on

fire?

Physical Therapy

2024

There's a fine dance when it all starts,
And then, over the course of time.

There's a fine dance
When it comes to
Pain
And
Numbness.

Need
Not too much heat
But also need
Not too much cold.

There's a fine dance when it comes to
Pain
And
Soreness,

And that itch—
It's *always* that itch—
In between.

There's a fine dance
Between

The pain
And
The pain
You need to heal.

Stronger
But not stronger than before.

Not stronger than before
But
Yes,

Stronger than before.

Now just in a different way
After.

Stronger than before,
Stronger than you believed.

There's a fine dance...

And you don't want either or
To take too much
Of the lead,
You don't want either or
To take too much
Of the ring,
You don't want either or
To take too much
Of the court,
Don't want either or

To take too much
Out of you,

Even the healing.

Because

What will happen now,

how to be lowKEE

Especially
When you've healed?

That's the test
That's more uncertain
Than being stitched
Then being unstitched.

That's the test
More uncertain
Than limbs being mended.

And that is the test
Of healing, and having to find out
Whether all of it really is mended,

Or if you ever will be
(Broken

Again.)

In this fine dance.

Sneakerhead, back to the game. Still gotta work on that dribble.

2024

No white.
That's a death sentence.
(Too much to maintain)

PINK?
That's a deaf sentence.
(TOO much of a tone to explain)

But maybe I've always been
Attracted to the trend
Of staying neutral:

A little white, pink,
Is aight, as long as it
Blends (in)

Like I'm used to.

A little white, a little pink
To let me know that I'm still
Feelin'

But not too much, too.

A little white, a little pink
As I work on my handle (on myself), my footing
To let me know
A slight veer and fall away
Can still be okay

'Cause this all just takes time getting used to.

A little white, a little pink
Possible to be

how to be lowKEE

Worn in
When

You
Still
Have
Feet.

So
Lace up.

School & Work

The early bird gets the worm,

and I get a way out of the 9 to 5 (even as remote)
2023

Night owls,

I know;
It's hard out here.

Just hold on
Just another full moon.
Maybe by morning,
We can sleep in
And still get paid.

Or maybe if we're really lucky,
We'll wake up to
An early retirement
And a bangin' stock portfolio that triplicated itself overnight.

But with even just a bit of luck,
We'll wake up
And aim for our goals yet again.

The Husband (Possibly) Has Erectile Dysfunction (But Luckily, Girl Bois Don't).

2023

No, not me. On both counts.
But that's what was told to me once during a work meeting. (Sidebar: I didn't work in a medical office.)
I get lucky like that with classified information.

That saying about some things are best kept to yourself?
Yeah, the people who come up with these things and then come up to me with them
Didn't get the memo.
Maybe the one above thought growing the news at work
Would help something else sporadically grow at home
As a result.

Sometimes, it's awkward. (Like above)
Sometimes, it makes a good pastime while waiting for time to quickly pass.
(Also, like above. Because, hey, it was almost the end of the work day.)
But most times, it's funny.

Until it isn't.

Because then you end up feeling some kind of way. (Like I did for the man above.)
He didn't ask for the—possible—ED, and he damn sure didn't ask for it to be talked about.)
Secondhand embarrassment.
Pity.
Or just a desire to—

"Girl bois."
See, now *you're* doing too much.
Because now, *I'm* a subject. (And sidebar: No, this wasn't a course elective.)
This time, outside of the college building during post-grad.

But still on campus, inside the new dorms.
Great idea as far as that: Our school was expanding into four years,
and many freshmen wanted a semblance of more freedom.

An unsolicited (possibly inebriated) idea on *this*: "I like them."
Girl. Why are you *still* telling me about girl bois? I have a name.
One I don't particularly love, but I'll claim that before
Girl bois?
"Yeah."

Yeah, I parrot back in my head.

Another bit of classified information.
And now, I've just added *that* to my girl boi files.
(Don't call me. I'll call you if I decide to take you up on that proposition.)

And with all of these insider deets
That I've accumulated over the years,
They all have further confirmed my belief:
Although you shouldn't hold everything close to the chest,
Doing so with some things
Is the best modus operandi.

Not because they're particularly embarrassing,
Or unnecessary,
Or borderline offensive.
But because
Being lowkey ain't too damn bad.

That way,
The times you do speak,
You (possibly) get a different result.

2015. Or was it '14?

2024

There once was a time
When someone called a student
Took a pause from the books
To go outside.

Chillin' in the back in leather,
No hoodie,
Acting like the music's too good for me

Because the one
In the fedora or Air Force 1s
Says I'm suave.

That was me,
And that I was
I suppose,
If we're judgin' promise and personality
By the clothes.
But roles
Are left to the stage
Left to the ones who get paid
For it.

Me, I was just acting class,
Yet another elective to my name,
And I paid
For it.

Fast forward to now,
With a degree or two to my name
Who have I become?

It's a question
That each day

Seems to break further and further away
In its run.

But one thing has remained
Since 2015,
Hasn't changed
Like the leather and hoodies
Or the friends.

And that's
That
My cool, my *'suave'*
Is still playin' bodyguard at the fence.

Waiting outside,
Waiting for the time
That I just might
Have my real graduation.

Because instead of jackin' my style,
Jackin' my accredited salary
They very well might just jack me.
Because in life, that's what I've grown to believe,
That I gotta be
On guard,
Always
That's the motif.
On guard,
Making sure when I finally graduate
That it's only for certain eyes to see.

When I finally graduate.

(Lowkey Fail #1) As I apply to this same role on LinkedIn from your company for the sixth time in these past 5 months...

2023

Y'all play too much.

And obviously, I'm childish (and broke), so...

2024 Update:
Legend, according to LinkedIn, has it that the job posting is still lurkin' out there.

All of us need to invest in real estate.

2020

A lot of us won't find real
Love.
Real
Connections.
Because we're not in real
Estate.

Wait.
I'll explain.

We have no idea of how to rehab
The houses we dwell in
With the old, rickety beds we've made and now lie in,
And no idea of how to then
Put them on the market and show them off to others.
(And no, pretty eyes or witty lines
Don't count because behind those cheap Dollar Store white curtain blinds,
Your inside
Is still a hot ass mess.
And even 100% prime silk curtains will start to unravel sooner or later.)

And it's all because we've decided to shut our doors
Or never fully opened them in the first place.

Closed them after heartbreaks,
Hardships, and life's other beatings
That tucked our tails and our trust deeper and deeper inside our homes,
And led us to make tainted commitments of forevers only to ourselves—
Our Hearts and Mistrust now newlywed.

Then we vowed to never open our front door again.
Off the market.
All of us living behind walls.

All of us need to invest in real estate.

Bad Habits

2024

Don't create a habit
Of screwing over others,

Because

It tends to have a habit
Of screwing over
You.

My ~~Beef~~ Situationship with Myers, Briggs and dem
2023

After thirteen tests
From about thirteen different sites
And 8 INFJ, 4 INFP, and 1 forced ISFP results later,
I'm none the more special,
None the more self-realized,
And still confused
About every damn thing.

But what I *have* realized
Is that I have an unreliable infatuation ~~to personality tests.~~

And doing the same thing while expecting different results
Is crazy.

Especially when you can just like the very first end result
From the start:
You

And who you've shaped up to be
Through all the tests
Life has given.

(Lowkey Fail #2) As I take another transfer from my business account to put into my personal checking account for the fifth time, for the first time ever, this year...

2023

I realize one thing:

I need that supposed sudden inheritance that the ruler of my 2nd house conjunct my Venus will bestow me, according to Tumblr.
Or this astrology ish is for the birds.

But even more,

It's hard out here, y'all.

I might have to become that early bird tryna get that worm. 🫠
If there's any left.

Inflation is hurting everything out here.*

*2024 Update:
Still waitin' on that inheritance.

Still Outside

Churches, Hoods, Bookstores, Prisons,
&
Other Hard Third Places

Things I still don't understand about this place now that I'm in my 30s
2023

1. How Twizzlers are still in production and why they ever went into production in the first place
   They don't feel like taste like rubber to the rest of y'all? (Don't ask me how I know what rubber tastes like.)

2. Daylight savings time
   Winter has the depressing aesthetic down to a science. It doesn't need fake science's wardrobe assistance.
   I vote for a daylight checkings. Daylight doesn't need to be saved; it needs to come save us (and our pockets, particularly after Black Friday and Christmas).

3. How I ever used to eat cantaloupe as a kid

4. And speaking of fruit,
   nature couldn't come up with some better fall/winter ones?

5. And speaking (again) of winter:
   Like, for real. Let's be so for real for a minute: How is it anyone's favorite season?

6. But lastly,
   if I'm such a picky consumer around candy and seasonal changes, why do I so easily accept the expectations placed upon me from others? Or even more, how do I continue to (let my) stomach (work against me and continue to buy into) it?

Wait, I lied.

And *why*
is Bobby short for Robert and not Robbie,
and Bill for William???

Tomorrow.

2023

I gotta keep going
Because if I don't
I'll realize I got lost a long time ago.

I gotta keep going
Because if I don't
I'll realize my battery went out,
Got lost a long time ago.

I gotta keep going
Because if I stop
I'll realize I stopped a long time ago.

Stopped going the right way
Stopped going any way,
Anywhere,
And lost any and every thing
A long time ago.

And if there's one thing
About time,
It's that once it's lost,
It's lost forever.
The yesterday, a long time ago,
The today, only a little time left,
And giving way to tomorrow.

...But wait...

To All My Frenemies

2023

It's not that I don't like people *per se*.
I just don't like their actions.

It's not so much the human
But the human's capabilities
To do a whole LOT,
Too much,
Too much of the time.
Because

Humans gonna human.

But *some*times...

Even I have to admit,
That isn't too bad.

Sometimes,
It's pretty good
Laughs,
Helping hands that appear out of thin air,
Poetry in motion like leaves touching your shoulder during the chill,
Memories in the making,
Or happy endings.

A good story
That you didn't want to farewell.

Because just like humans gonna human,

Time is gonna time.

how to be lowKEE

And before it slips away,
You gotta make the most.
Of the bad

And the good.

I, a fellow (*sigh*) human,
Wish that for you.
And for me, too.
So, you fools betta wish me the same.

Because I know how y'all roll.

Today, y'all finally got the homie outside. (For a lil bit)

2023

And immediately, I wanted to go back in.

Immediately, I knew this was a bad idea because

I actually kicked it for a little bit.

I actually laughed a little bit.

Damn, I actually even *vibed* a little bit.

And it made me realize

I wanted a little bit more

Of a lot of it

To take home.

'Cause y'all know about us Black people and our to-go plates,

(It means it *has* to be some type of holiday.)

Especially when we don't come outside (enough),

When we don't talk (enough).

Not even

A little bit

It's Your World
2024

If your world ends
Whenever someone else leaves,
Was it ever really your world,
Or were you camped out in their orbit?

If your world ends
Whenever someone else leaves,
Was it ever a place to exist?

Or if your world ends
Maybe your world isn't big enough, not even for you,
Or your world,
So many pieces
Of it,
Have been added to
So many
Other solar systems,

Making your world
Much more
Valuable,
Special
Than you ever took the time to realize,
Know.

Because if you did,
You wouldn't let it
Go
And
Go

Until there is none of it left.

Treasure

2024

Dig deep.

Deep,
Deep,

Until you finally
Get there.

And once you finally
Do, let me know.

Not because I want in
On some of
That treasure,

But because
It will be good enough for me
To see
That look on your face
Once *you* see
All of that treasure

That's *been* down there
Still waiting for you,
Still left
After all this time.

Here's a (Magic) Trick.
2023

**Don't be afraid
To be afraid.**

That's when the magic starts.

Are You Afraid of the Dark?

2024

When I was younger.

But even more, afraid of
Goosebumps

That come out of nowhere.
On the back of your neck,
Standing up on high alert on your arms

When you think
Someone's there with you
In the dark.

Not because they're suddenly there with you,
But because you're surprised
That they're
There *with*
You

In the dark.

Because often, we fear
Letting others in
Because often, we feel we're
Too "dark."

Leaving us all
In the dark
About the person who might be next to us,
Who might have always been
Right
Next
To

how to be lowKEE

You.

(Now, Here's a Dare)devil's Mantra.

2023

And if you've never been afraid,
I have a question:

Where have you been
Or have you already been

Through it all?

When you can answer to that last part,
Then you'll be able to answer to the first
And see that being first,
It was the least scary
Of it all.

We Light

2024

When you see us, don't worry;
We don't bite.

We only light
Get lit
Get blunts lit
Get lit
Up

But if we were to ever let that
Light
Up
In our heads
Equally shine,
We'd finally see that

Our light
Is enough

Has always been

A noun
That doesn't need a verb
Especially when

It puts us into a sentence.

Turn the page.

2023

Let a chapter
Be a chapter
If (when) it needs to be.
And then

--Your favorite TikToker, probably (*Autumn, Winter, Tax*)

2024 (But more like Autumn of 2023, 2024, 2025, and at this rate, 2026)

Be like the leaves in the fall.

When they do,

They do so with an enviable coordination,

A bold flair to the emerging bare,

And an indomitable return.

Which is much more than I can say
About my aspirations and my pockets.

So, hope you got more out of this than I did (or ever will probably),
Or whatever.

But in all honesty,
If this doesn't influence you in any other way,
I hope it at least inspires you to
Show who's boss
In every single season that awaits you.

Even tax season.

Politricks / Whatever You Wanna Call It, Just Call It.

2024

Okay, I'm not into politics,
But let's call it what it is.

I know about the branches of government,
But I know even more about
How the branches of the tree
Can't be a tree
Without its root.

I don't know it all about politics,
But I know about
How we often don't care about that root
Until the root begins to
Demand or experience an uproot
ing.

I don't know it all about politics,
But I know enough about the economics
Of
Auto repairs, MLM invites from high school classmates
I had last spoken to in
High school,
Of
Give and take,
And give or take,
And give and give against take and take,
Of
demanding more from everyone else
And the cost it takes from our self.

I'm not into politics,
But I know about the wars in Gaza,
Ukraine, nations in Africa,
As much as the wars within

how to be lowKEE

Us.

I'm not into politics,
But I know how everyone else's problem
Isn't our problem
Until it hits

Too close to home.

You can call it
Politics, politricks,
Or something else,
But I'm calling it what it is:

There isn't any greater trick
Than the one we pull on ourselves,

When we think doing anything
Else
But governing ourselves, controlling ourselves first
Will help us stay on top
Of anything
But the debris, litter, and dirt
Awaiting us
Every time we rip up
And rip off.

--Some Al Capone type, probably (*Writer's Block*)

2024

I been around the block a few times.

And it didn't take me too long to figure out

That the block only goes for so long.

Those on my block growing up
On Southside Chicago told me that.

But they didn't exactly say it in words.

They said it in their faces:
Many of them, no more than two decades old,
Some of them, looking decades old
Even if their biological age said otherwise.

Back in 2022, I drove by that place
And wondered how it ever looked like such a big world
To me.

Yeah,
the block really isn't that damn long.

I learned that in those faces
On that block.
Some of them had a slow, watchful scope
Of their block,
Seeing one end of the street to one end
And seeing the other side of the street to the other,
All without ever turning their head.

Those were the select few
Who'd been on that block the longest,
Even if their faces
Showed different.
Many more should've paid attention
To those faces.
Probably would've made it on the block longer.

But instead, many of them turned their heads in one way,
A check on that block
For police,
Or the even bigger enemy,
Another gang rival,
As they slipped a hit
Or a bag of a fix.

And by leaving their backs exposed the other way,
Either or of the above
Got them

Off that block.

Finally,
Off that block.

But not ever in the way they wanted.

Or sometimes,
I think it was what they wanted.

To get off that block
By any means:
Their body planted just inches off its curb,
Whether it would mean
In handcuffs
Or
In bullets.
Because they knew it

Only went for so long.

Much like
Their lives.

Much like

Us all.

Gotta be quiet, gotta be good

just like sugar
2023

They say being sick is like its own trauma.
(People say a lot of things.)

Like the one mid-to-late Chicago winter in early 2023
When I went to go visit my great-auntie,
(On) My mother's side,
(On) My most enigmatic side.
And on her stronger, non-arthritic-ravaged, diabetes-caused side

That didn't feel as pained to lift, move,
As she lay in her 'end of life' bed
Post-release,
She looked from one face in the room,
To the second,
To me

And said,
"You're too loud.
Gonna get us in trouble.
Don't worry;
I'll be quiet, I'll be good."

That doesn't sound like someone wanting end of life to me.

Sounds like she wants to be quiet, to be
Good.
Sounds like that's what she thinks she needs
To do to live,
Or else she'll die.
That's what will get her, not the sugar levels on high.
And that makes me wonder if that's the sugar talkin'.

And then, I wonder if that's the same kind

That fueled our whispered, wet, wounded talks
Out in the sugarcane fields:
Told to keep quiet,
Don't tell our tales.
Told to be good.
Keep goin' on like nothing is wrong.

But by getting *too* quiet,
In those whispers,
That *can't* be good
For those profiting off
Our blood
Sugar:

Means
We're either dying
Or
Thinking
About how better we want to live.
Yeah, something's surely up,
Surely wrong
Once that sugar revs up,
Kicks in.

Listen:

"You're too loud,
Gonna get us in trouble.
Don't worry;
I'll be quiet, I'll be good."

But you listen this time,
No, not you, auntie.

You.

how to be lowKEE

I don't want to be quiet.
I no longer want to be good.
I want to be bad.
Mad.
Like the one trapped inside.
I want, have to punch bags,
Strike until I can no longer feel my
Calloused fisted knuckles.
Work out til I
No longer feel my body,

Work out til I
Forget I had one.

Like how your leg quietly, slowly falls asleep,
No longer can assist you (to move)
When too much weight on it bears on it for too long.

That's the same thing with auntie's arm.
That's the same thing that happens to your soul
When you've been bearing it to be good, quiet for too long.

That's why she has bed sores.

No, not me.
My auntie.
She wants to get up,
But days before
She wanted to get *out*.

It's a complex thing,
Movement: trying to be and another part, trying to be
Somewhere else
Like a sugar coma suddenly seeping in—
But I understand her.
That's me most days,
Even though I don't have exactly what she has.
But I have a commonality, next of kin, blood:

76

Sugar.
Maybe I should've asked for some
Sugar
To be quiet, good
Instead of the books I did after one Fourth of July
Back in '99.
Because the latter you can't eat,
Can't find sweetness,
The sweetness I desired at seven at that time.

That we all desire at that time,
As kids
And that only gets stronger once we're big
And now told
Not just to be quiet, good,
But also to get up, and get out,
and
Grow up,
And
Act like nothing ever happened.

Yeah, just cut off the limb
After having too much sugar
From the ice pops at the beach that fateful July 4th day,
From my uncle's glazed gaze back at that fateful place,
Yes, even from...
Those shiny five dollar paperbacks at the store on the way
Back home

And on all of the pages
In all of the books
The uncle said,
"Quiet.

Good."

So quiet

That I didn't hear the car wheels turn
Down to my neighborhood street,
So quiet
Because I was reading
All of that sugar
That had been prescribed to me.

Making my memory my lost limb.
Made me forget
It actually happened
In the sour way it did,
Made me forget
For many years, the year of age I'd actually been when
It did,
Made me forget
I, in fact, fell victim to it:
The sugar
Like my auntie.
She knew it,
She saw it
In me. And so,
She
Reminded me
Of it:

"You're too loud,
Gonna get us in trouble."

Of the risk I was about to do.

Even though I didn't even speak.
And I saw the fear and sadness
In her
Eyes, as she, even in her own sugar high,
Even still, spotted what was coming through..

"Don't worry."

...In the silence whispering from my eyes
To hers, too...

"I'm good."

I tried to convince what had become just the two of us in the room.

And even, after all these years, as I finally, slowly awake,
I still wonder if that's the sugar talkin',
Or the sugar talkin' to the trauma,
Or the trauma itself that we tried to sweeten up with the help of it.
Because one thing about sugar that we learn even while still kids:

Too much of it,
That sugar,

And
You
Get more than double vision.
You
Also

Get sick.

Things I've Learned About This Mad Crazy Rollercoaster

2020 (And the update as of 2024)

Called life so far:

1. First things first. No, you don't get a safety belt, so you better hold tight, toughen up, and make it through the ride alive. Or let go, give up, and be whipped out into the air to never be seen again.

2. Life is more accurately the School of Hard Knocks. Or the other way we metaphorically look at it, this crazy, unhinged rollercoaster is just the fun 'recess.' You know just for some shits and giggles for the daredevils out there.

3. Sometimes your golden birthday ain't so golden. It's cool, you just have more awesome ones in store. You're just saving up your gold tokens like they do in the video games.

4. Contrary to what the costumes you might've used to wear as a kid (And for many of you, still do. And we're not just talking Halloween.) have gassed you up into erroneously believing,

   you are not a superhero.

   Let me explain.

   Not everyone wants to be saved. Not everyone *needs* to be saved; at least, not according to your beliefs and your thought that you can give them an upgrade whether emotionally, spiritually, physically, financially, romantically, or all of the above. Not everyone is interested in being the damsel in distress or fallen/lost soldier to your thought and belief system. Why? Because they have their own and, in their minds, they might be the next big thing, living their best lives. And for them, they *are*. If they're happy in their land of ignorance or stagnation and don't want to join your community, so be it. Who's to say that your land of maturity, growth, and change is not really the land of hell or bondage or monotony? At least based on what they're looking at right now when they look at you. Maybe they see your grass on the other side and guess what? They *don't* think it looks greener. Or maybe they do, but they prefer their brown, struggling lawn more. Some people just aren't horticulturalists or born with a green thumb—and don't care to be either. Sometimes you have to widen your perspective, step out of your own damn green front yard. What might work for you as a single person, doesn't automatically work for everyone else. Your idea of happiness might be someone else's idea of captivity or boredom. So, accept it and fly on by, Superman (and Superwoman).

   Who knows? Maybe (keyword, maybe, just to soothe your ego a bit) this is just not their season for their rescue. Maybe they don't appear in your hero story until Season 3 (or 4 or 5) or until the sequel arriving in the next few years. So, in the meantime, like I said:

   Fly on by, Superman(/woman). You have other lives to tend to, including your own.

5. Tough love can come from yourself. Yes, and it can hurt just as much, or even more, than that given to you by others. Point blank, it can hurt like hell. (And this is not just something the athletes and fitness buffs know.) Owning up to your own BS when no one else will continue to fall for it anymore (or never did). Uncovering all of the old, unhealed hard stories you've buried into your mind and finally admitting

to them being the subconscious reason for a lot of your present hard stories: screw ups, ego trips, and stagnation that you have to heal once and for all, no matter the discomfort. Giving yourself the hard pep talk to get your butt up and get what you need to get done, change what you need to change.

As the saying goes, sometimes, you just have to pick yourself up by the bootstraps. And that can be the hardest part.

But it's also the most rewarding part.

6. And finally, I've learned that I've learned some things, haven't learned most, and there will forever be more to learn that I might never know.

7. But sometimes, it's better not to know.

8. Because if you go looking for dirt to dig up, most times you'll find it.

9. And I don't know about you, but the older I get, the more I'm getting like my mom. And that means I'm very serious about keeping a clean home.

Small Towns

2024

They're a polarizing thing.

Small towns.

Some people love them,
Living in them.
Small towns.

Others live in them,
But hate them.
Small towns.

And the only fine line to separate
Is a fine line, territory.

Don't like it,
Move out.

Do like it,
Move in,
Stay in.

Small towns.

I've moved in
To one.
But five months in,
I've realized more than not fully being enamored,
I'm not fully enamored because I've *been*
In my own kind of

Small town.

Wasn't quite as rural,
But was just as stifling,
Just as south,
Down there.

It's always south

Even if it's not,
It feels like it.

Down there.

Seen this scene before,
Felt this before,
Down there.
Over and over again.

More irritating than
Continuously having my elbow bumped
By the passenger next to me
On the flight in

To this small town.

More irritated than
The rental car service rep
Giving me southern 'pleasantries'
Once I landed in

To this small town.

More irritated than
Being from the city
And an infestation forcing me
To once again, move in

to
This small town.

More irritated than
Being irritated that I *still*
Can't do or get something right
After all this time here,
More irritated than
Being irritated that I
Continuously
Allow myself to still be here
In

This small town.

Because anger shouldn't so easily
Suffocate you, communicate over you
Over and over again,
Not even in

A small town.

But the beautiful thing about
Small towns,
If we'd just take the time to appreciate it,
Socialize with it,
Live in it
Even if for just a while,
Just go there and just take time
To briefly visit it
Rather than dwell on it
With tired, forced, uneasy, or tight smiles,

We'd see that
What's even more intrusive yet heartening than the familiar faces
Of many
Is the familiar face
Of one,
Who forces you to rub elbows with it,
Become pleasant with it,

Even if you don't always want to.
But it's easy to

In a town
Of
One.

"I'll Pray for You."

2024

Those are the subtle
Not-so-subtle words spoken to us
Outlaws
As we await our trial
We've already seemed to be placed on.

"I'll pray for you,"
Is said to me by someone
Living up in that righteous place
As I live below in this hellish place they say
I chose.

And
"I'll pray for *you*..."
Now silently escapes me to the one...

"...As you fall down a ditch..."
...I decided to take off trial...

"...So, I can bury you."
In nothing but the artifacts of the crime chosen that day,
In those very same clothes.

"I'll pray for you,"
Has finally escaped me.

"Like you prayed for me..."
It's just the just thing to do...

"...At my burial where you held the shovel."

And like a wish, hoping it comes true.

Driving Lessons

2024

For each of us,

Different,

But the same:

A mix of tension, expectations,
And all of the various relations
That come from it,
From us mixed with those riding with us
Or trying to drive for us
While we try to drive.

Just trying to drive

In these sometimes tight spaces,
In our own lanes.

My niece was the other day,
So I went out with her
And taught her as much as I could
About what to do as the driver
Of her road.

But do it as tips,
Options,

Not as law,
Even in this experience where
We're
All the same,
Drivers navigating
The rules
Of the road.

Yeah, I take it easy
On my niece.
She in some ways
Reminds me
Of me
A bit in how she drives at that stage,
In how she navigates.
So, I take it easy.

Just take it easy

In these sometimes tight spaces,
In our own lanes

As my mom says,
You can't drive mine
And yours at the same time.

But many try to.

Like my mom,

And my sister,
And damn—
But did my cousin really just get in here, too??

All prying at that steering wheel
Of my car
Of my road.

And it all
Started a moment ago,
Cutting just a moment ago

Between me and my niece.
Just a moment that was supposed to be

KEELA BUFORD

A driving lesson.

Sigh
Here they are, taking the wheel.

Now, how the *hell* did we just make *this* turn?
When at first, we were just talking about
Colors,
Colors we all think we look best in?

Just before hitting the road with my niece,
We were literally
Just
Talking
About
Colors.
Wait...
That's what did me in.

Too many colors, loud,
Too proud,
Dangerous for the driver, me
And my niece,
I guess
They guessed.

So, they took that sign
As their sign
To take that wheel
As their wheel,
And now,

They're driving

A point:
"She said, 'Hey, beautiful' to me! Then I said, hi, without even thinking.
You think she thinks that's a sign!!"
"Ugh, was she hard in the face and aggressive, like an ugly pit?

That's *always* a sign."
"Then my mom was even worse than me. 'I can't STAND that!
Always pushin' themselves on others, misinterpreting.
Not everyone wants to live that way!'"

And I'm not trying to drive this way.

But suddenly,
They're driving,
Pushed me right out of the driver's seat.
Misinterpreting one conversation,
Colors and those which we like the
Same,
As a segue to another:
No, too many colors are too loud, too
Different.

So we're changing lanes.

They're driving,
And I'm just riding.

They won't even look at me,
Even while giving me the rules
In my own damn car.

But I understand;
I'm in the backseat

Of my own damn car.

As I wonder how my niece escaped,
My sister's trying to drive me in one direction,
My mom, naturally,
And now, my cousin in the mix, too.
In my car

Driving it on home.

They're drivin'

And I ride,
As I wonder
When

This drive will end.

Drive It on **Home**

how to be lowKEE

And I Believed That, Too.

2010

Growing up, I used to tap dance...

In corrective shoes.
Soles tapping the ceramic tiles in that two-flat kitchen
In syncopation with the faucet,
That would always host its own performance
In the sink.

The spoons and plates,
Oven and fridge, pots and pans
The only audience I thought I could ever need,
Always sitting in their assigned seats,
Idle.
Never interrupting

My pigeon-toed blues.

Expressed through
Pitter-patters
In the melody of quick, varied rhythms,
Sometimes going off the straight and narrow,
Wayward.
In my pigeon-toed shoes.

My mind reassured me that it was
Cool.
My mind reassured me that I was
A star,

And I believed it.

The only one who could
Convince me otherwise was
Myself.

Confession time...

2023

I wrote sixty-five percent of this book while chilling in my bed.

Don't judge
'Cause I got it like that.

I'm a late bloomer

2020 (Update as of 2024)

Much like I'm a late riser
Out of bed,
Which is fine.

But don't let everyone step over your burgeoning garden bed
So much
To the point that you forget
You were supposed to be a flower.

Don't ever
Forget that
Sometimes petals of wisdom
Take time to break out
And shout out about
What they know
Through their long, colorful stretches
Once they finally emerge,
Made up of rain, sun, rain, sun.
Rain.

Rain, sun, rain, sun,
Rain.

That's the season
Deeper than the seasons.
That's the process
That can't be rushed too soon.

I just had to take more time
In my process.
Some people's water season is known as spring;
Mine was a monsoon.

Being one part sheltered,

how to be lowKEE

Being one part scared,
Being one part stubborn,
My petals,
My wisdom,
My lessons
Needed more rain
To taste.

I'm just a late
Bloomer,
Who finally realized the petals,
And why they took time.

And why it was perfectly fine.

And then finally, I
No longer needed another taste
Of rain.

I Remember

2023

...Not a lot, actually.
From childhood.
Even teenagehood.
Not even...

You see where this is going.

Good, at least someone does. (Proud of ya, really.)
Because it's a bit trickier for me.

Can't see where you're going (or trying to get to)
If you can't always clearly see where you used to be (or what you're trying to get away from).
Need a starting point (painful motivation)
For a finish line (triumphant accomplishment).

Can't see what will possibly be
If you don't even know what was.

That's why I always have to be reminded:
"Hey, remember that time your momma
Woke up that night of your birthday
And saw your friend and her sisters laid up in
The living room with us boy cousins?"

About anything:
"You *did* have summer reading in high school."
"No...just grammar school."
Wait, you don't even remember your childhood. Remember?

And *every*thing:
"See...That's why you have to start talking to someone about all of it..."

Even sometimes, my own face:
"You look like him."

"...I do?" 'Cause last time I checked, it's always been my mom.

But hey, I *do* always have to be reminded.

"Yep. Go off to yourself and everything. All him." Reminded that I'm a Buford.

From on my side.

"Yep! In that chin, too!"

And on his side, too.

Can't get past that.

Your blood. Your (physical...and psychological) ties.

Your past.

Even if you can't always recall all of it. (Or don't want to.)

Only just a handful of times:

A glimpse at a church here. (A funeral...Not mine. But if it were, of course, I wouldn't have remembered. Ha.)

An awkward hug,

Then a random look that two strangers could've made more heartwarming there. (A graduation...Nope again. But hey, probably wouldn't have remembered that either, anyway.)

And that's why I never got a chance to confirm at least one of those reminded recollections:

Never looked at the chin.

Then, comes a second funeral. (Not mine. His.)

Summer of 2022. (That I didn't attend. Not because I forgot it. No one gave me a chance to. But because a greater father figure's, my mom's dad, was the month before.)

Then I remember.

A question everyone asked

With their eyes

Rather than their mouths,

With the thoughts in the silence

Rather than the light ones spoken:

How are you grieving?

How am I what? Not remembering my past, a part of it? Because it never was? That's a damn good question.

And so, I said with my hesitant half-smile,

The one we give when we're either grieving and hiding it,
Or not really recalling something—
And hiding it.
And in that "smile" that sometimes I wonder if it might
Truly resemble his at times, all in that mouth area.
In that smile above *that* body part, I "said":
"Yeah.
I grieve
What never was
And now, what never will be."

Easy to do when the past has only visited you a handful of conscious times
And the rest stay trapped (maybe or maybe not purposely) in the subconscious.

Easy to do when
You never went to the funeral
For the one you never really knew
Because he never really knew you
Or tried to.

That's what I remember
And always will.

And then,
That's when
I remember (one final thing):

Why I try not to.

Just one more bottle.
Put baby to sleep.
2023

For all of us fighting something more,
Or trying to swallow it all down,
Or both.

One after the other.

It's time for us to stand up and walk.

Growing Old Is a Blessing.

2024

It has its perks
Like

Forgetting things.

Sometimes,
It's for the best.

Yeah, you'll forget
Some memories,
But those were probably unremarkable
Anyway.

Yeah, you might forget
Most memories,
But the ones
That really stood out to you,
Made you smile,
Made it for this long haul so far,
Stay with you.

Sometimes,
For the long haul.
Sometimes,
It's more than remarkable.
Sometimes,
It's
Forever.

And that's even better
Than
...
Than...

how to be lowKEE

Forgetting.

These are a few of my favorite things.

2023

1. Being cold in bed but not wanting to become even colder while going to turn up the heat (which will, in turn, turn up your gas bill)

2. Finally obtaining *that* comfortable position in bed only to realize you have to go get something.

   Or pee.
   Usually, it's to go pee.

3. Jumping into the shower only to realize you moved so fast that you forgot your towel

4. Being asked the last time you inserted a Playtex or Kotex into your pants and who else might've recently joined the party down there (to only then be looked at like 😵 when you came in like 🚶 🧔 rather than like 🚶 🧑🏿 even though the patient intake form you filled out was like ✖ ✖ 🪪) when all you wanted to do was get your blood drawn.

5. The two (and sometimes, three) back-to-back ads that appear before and within every other YouTube video because you're too cheap to get Premium.

6. Musicals that think it's a perfect time for a song and dance routine every time a person cries, enters the room, and/or inhales

   Excluding *The Wiz* (the original). That one's off-limits. I actually really like that one.

7. Cookies being a bad influence and tempting you all up and down the internet to buy those pairs of Nikes you should've never clicked on in the first place.

8. Trying to go back to sleep while you still can
   But not being able to
   And having to finally accept the fact that
   Maybe it's just time
   To finally get the hell up.

And get all the worms that have been waiting for you.

Sugar. The Quality Kind.

2024

Something like
Agave,
Not stevia.
Something like
Sweet potato
Pie,
Maple,
Or coconut
Sugar
For me.

That's all I need
To sweeten my treat.

Sometimes, it was a package
Of chocolate chip cookies,
Many more times,
Vanilla wafers left up on the standup freezer
In a bin.
The generic kind,
But that's always the best kind: universal sweetness
Of pure sugar,
The same one my cousins and I grew up with

Over years and years
Until I could see it eye to eye,
Easy to reach.

Easy to access,
Easy to love.
But of course, it was
When it was
Always sweet.

Even when I'm more maple these days,
Sugar will always
Be the generic, standard kind,
The universal sweet
Like those found in
Those old-fashioned family movies and series

On an easy Sunday morning:
The smile greeting you on visits to brighten your stay,
Even better with some Harold's Chicken
Heavy on the mild sauce with "friers," the large size, by mid-day,
A ride-along summer drive, quality time
In a car whose seats were covered in duct tape,
Sticking to you for a bit,
Then dissolving away.
Like
A parting hug to make it alright
Even though it couldn't stay.
A kind chuckle, sweet,
Fading away.

That's the sugar
I did need.

Because what I've come to realize
Is that we all need
A lil sugar,
No matter the variety,
So long as it's sweet.
We all need
A lil sugar,
Just the quality kind.

And that's what my
Grandpa
Was to me.

A Homage to Some Greats I Know (Including a Keeshond and a Scar)

2024

If you're a dog person
Or a cat person,

It says a lot about you.

What it says about me
Is that I had a dog named Ashley,
And she's the reason I don't think
I can go through
Having another dog again.
Shared parts of the same name as me,
her a Keeshond, me a Kee.
Grew up with me
Since the age of three.
Grew up with me
Through height peaks and flat Chicago streets.

What it says about me
Is that childhood had its good times, fun times
But also its bad times
As I was getting older in age:

Lost parts of me,
Like my Granny,
And eventually,
Ashley, too.

But before that,
There were falls:
Like Granny
Onto the front lawn with age,
Like Ashley,
Years later, down the basement stairs with age,
And like me

Accidentally
Landing on her, too.

The proof comes in my scar.

And it's sometimes not our fault
Or a moment to dwell on
When we fall;

We can get back up.

I have.

We can get back up.

Ashley tried to,
Granny, too (scars on her chest to prove it).

And did
Many times
Before the last time
When she couldn't

And had to take her rest.
And that's okay, too.

Especially if we've been at war,
And have scars
To prove it
And to prove to ourselves

We're still here (including maybe for the ones who can no longer be,
Including maybe our own old selves),
And we're still joyful (especially after surviving war),
And we're still alive (maybe now, just a bit different).

That's who we are as a person,

how to be lowKEE

No matter if a dog person
Or a cat person;

The proof comes in our scars.

Forgiveness can be the hardest thing.

2023

I don't know who needs to hear this, but:

Forgive

Yourself.

Because

I forgive you.

- Your inner child,

Or your age of your greatest 'F up,'

Or

Whoever you were

At whatever given point in time

When this all began.

Just thought y'all should know... (Confession time 2 ✌️)

2023

Like my niece tried to do with her Chick-fil-A job four weeks in,
I'm writing this formal letter of resignation
Because y'all are a piece of work,
And I don't get paid enough for this ish.

Plus, the astro fam over on Tumblr turned out to be right, so...

Best,
Tired asl

The End

of a Long Year

how to be lowKEE

2024

As a leftie,
Over the years, I've learned of the many things
I can't do:

Can't exist
In the middle
At the seat at the table,
Have to be on the outside,

Can't write
Without a smear
Or two on my hand's side,

Without stains
All kinds,
Including tears,

From pains
All kinds,
Including years

Of setting the table for,
Continuously irritating the skin for
Memories that have overstayed their visit.
One minute, day, or weekend in time becoming fifty-two in a year
That soon became another
Until all the years have felt like one.

But like all visits,
Visitors,
Still,
They must go.

Once sandwiched in the middle,
Trapped in pains and stains,
And bumping against, spilling out

Me at the most inopportune times,
So that eventually, they'd finally reach this point in time
Where they fall off the edge.

But of course, they need to
When I need to
Write.

Need the elbow room,
The grace
To embrace
Being a leftie.

Even when at times,
It's made some situations
Ones I had to navigate a bit differently,
My quote unquote liability.

And knowing that a handicap
Doesn't have to be a crutch.

Sometimes, it can be a superpower
To conquer the world
A little bit better than most
When you're one of the few
Who has been doing it your entire life.

And maybe I can't write all of the things
That have happened to me as a leftie.
Maybe I can't right all of the things
That I've done since then because of it.

Because all of those memories can't be undone.

But *this*,

how to be lowKEE

Right now,
Is a damn good start.

Because
You
Don't have to
Stay low
After falling off the edge
Of the table,
Onto the curbside,
When
You
Always
Held the key.

Did you make it to your
new place? Share with us.

KEELA BUFORD
is the author of *Pride, and Joy*
(yes, the comma is intentional),
somewhat like the historical sister novel to her second
novel, *The Buy-In*. She is a content specialist who has
helped many businesses in vast
industries. Her creative and screenplay works have placed
in semifinalist positions with Stage 32, WeScreenplay,
Outfest, and IndieFEST.